Soccer Practice

A Comprehensive Handbook Covering 14 Areas for Smart Soccer Players, Coaches, and Parents - Step-by-Step

Table of Contents

Preface

This book was written to change the way players think about and play the game of soccer. I struggled for years with sub-average performances as a defender, defensive center midfielder, and outside midfielder. I was often placed in these positions because I could not score. Due to my immaturity, I did not like others correcting my form. I knew it needed considerable improvement, so I would take it personally when someone gave me feedback. I realized that this was limiting my ability to become the player I wanted to be.

Therefore, I sought out the knowledge that allowed me to score multiple goals a game, defend correctly, pass with excellent form, etc. As a result of this success, I could not help but share my understanding of the game to other players who are looking to improve, parents who want to boost their child's confidence on the field, and coaches who want to be viewed as outstanding by all of their players and their players' parents. Though I train players individually and in small groups, I know that writing the information down in a book will allow it to reach more eyes, build more confidence, and make a significant impact on the world.

This book dives deep into the important topics of soccer. Though the correct form and tactics are extremely helpful in ensuring the ball ends up in the opponent's net, you also need a strong mindset to improve on any weaknesses, solidify your strengths, and implement many tips and tricks, to become the person on your team that consistently scores.

This book will help you become the most admired player on your team. Changing one or two things may help you become better, but once you start implementing most or even all the techniques described in this book, you will see a significant improvement in your performance on the field. However, remember that the knowledge in this book is only helpful when applied. You must apply it to score 10X more goals each season, which will lead to several more wins.

INDIVIDUAL SOCCER PLAYER'S PYRAMID

In the image, the most critical field-specific skills to work on are at the base of the Individual Soccer Player's Pyramid. The pyramid is a quality outline to improve an individual soccer player's game. All the elements in the pyramid and the items surrounding it play a meaningful part in becoming a better player, but certain skills should be read and mastered first before moving on to the others.

You will notice that passing and receiving is at the foundation of the pyramid. This is because if you can receive and make a pass in soccer, then you will be a useful teammate. Even though you may not consistently score, dispossess the other team, or dribble through several opponents, you will still have the fundamental tools needed to play the sport and contribute to your team.

As you move one layer up, you find yourself with a decision to make on how to progress. Specifically, the pyramid is created with you in mind because each soccer player and each soccer position has different needs. Therefore, your choice regarding which path to take first is dictated by the position you play and more importantly, by the position that you want to play. In soccer and life, just because you are in a particular spot, position, or even a job, it does not mean that you have to stay there forever if that is not your choice. However, it is not recommended to refuse playing a position if you are not in the exact role you want. It takes time to develop the skills that will allow you to make a shift from one position to another.

If you want to become a forward, then consider starting your route on the second layer of the pyramid with shooting and finishing. As your abilities to shoot increase, your coach will notice your new finishing skills and will be more likely to move you up the field (if you are not a forward already). Be sure to communicate to the coach that you desire to be moved up the field to a more offensive position, which will increase your chances, as well. If you are already a forward, then dive deep into this topic to ensure you become the leading scorer; first on your team, and then in the entire league. Notice that shooting and finishing is considered less critical than passing and receiving. This is because you have to pass the ball up the field before you can take a shot on net.

Otherwise, you can start by progressing to dribbling & foot skills from passing & receiving because the proper technique is crucial to dribble the ball well. It is often necessary for a soccer player to use a skill to protect the ball from the other team or to advance the ball up the field to place their team in a favorable situation to score. The selection of this route is often taken first by midfielders and occasionally by forwards.

Defending is another option of how you can proceed from passing and receiving. Being able to keep the other team off the scoreboard is not an easy task. Developing a defender's mindset, learning which way to push a forward, understanding how to position your body, knowing when to foul, and using the correct form for headers is critical to a defender on the back line looking to prevent goals.

Finish all three areas in the second layer of the pyramid before progressing up the pyramid. Dribbling and defending the ball (not just shooting) are useful for an attacker; shooting and defending (not just dribbling) are helpful for a midfielder, while shooting and dribbling (not just defending) are helpful for a defender. Having a well-rounded knowledge of the skills needed for the different positions is important for all soccer players. It is especially essential for those soccer players who are looking to change positions in the future. Shooting and finishing, dribbling and foot skills, and defending are oftentimes more beneficial for soccer players to learn first, so focus on these before spending time on the upper areas of the pyramid. In addition, reading about each of these areas will help you to understand what your opponent wants to do.

Once you have improved your skills in the first and second tiers of the pyramid, move up to fitness. It is difficult to go through a passing/dribbling/finishing drill for a few minutes without being out of breath. However, as you practice everything below the fitness category in the pyramid, your fitness and strength will naturally increase. Performing technical drills allows soccer players to increase their fitness naturally. This reduces the need to focus exclusively on running for fitness.

Coming from the perspective of both a soccer player and trainer, I know that constantly focusing on running is not as fulfilling and does not create long-lasting improvements, whereas emphasizing shooting capabilities, foot skills, and defending knowledge creates long-lasting change. Often, coaches who focus on running their players in practice are also coaches who want to improve their team but have limited knowledge of many of the soccer-specific topics that would quickly increase their players' abilities. Not only does fitness in soccer include your endurance; it also addresses your ability to run with agility and speed and to develop strength and power, while using stretching to improve your flexibility. All these tools put together leads to a well-rounded soccer player.

Similar to the tier below it, you should focus on the fitness areas that will help you specifically, while keeping all of the topics in mind. For example, you may be a smaller soccer player who could use some size. In this case, you should emphasize weight training so that you can gain the muscle needed to avoid being pushed off the ball. However, you should still stretch before and after a lifting workout or soccer practice/game to ensure that you stay limber and flexible to recover quickly and avoid injuries.

Maybe you are a soccer player in your 20s, 30s, or 40s. Then, emphasizing your flexibility would do a world of good to ensure you keep playing soccer for many more years. However, doing a few sets of push-ups, pull-ups, squats, lunges, sit-ups, etc. per week will help you maintain or gain a desirable physique.

Furthermore, you could be in the prime of your career in high school, college, or at the pro level, which means that obtaining the speed and endurance needed to run for 90+ minutes is the most essential key to continue pursuing your soccer aspirations.

Finally, we travel to the top of the pyramid, which involves tryouts. Although tryouts occur only 1-2 times per year, they have a huge impact on whether you will make the team or get left out of the lineup. Tryouts can cause intense anxiety if you do not know the keys to make sure that you stand out from your competitors and are very confident from the start. These keys are explained in the Understand Soccer series book, *Soccer Tryouts: A Step-by-Step Guide on How to Easily Make the Team.*

The last portion of the pyramid are the areas that surround the pyramid. Though these are not skills and topics that can be addressed by your physical abilities, they each play key roles in rounding out a complete soccer player. For example, having a supportive parent/guardian or two is beneficial for transporting the child to games, providing the equipment needed, the fees for the team, expenses for individual training, and encouragement. Having a quality coach will help the individual learn how their performance and skills fit into the team's big picture.

Sleeping enough is critical to having enough energy during practices and on game days, in addition to recovering from training and games. Appropriate soccer nutrition will increase a soccer player's energy and endurance, help them achieve the ideal physique, and significantly aid in their recovery.

Understanding soccer positions will help you determine if a specific role is well-suited for your skills. It is important to know that there are additional types of specific positions—not just forwards, midfielders, and defenders. A former or current professional player in the same position as you can provide guidance on the requirements to effectively play that position.

Finally, you must develop a mindset that will leave you unshakable. This mindset will help you prepare for game situations, learn how to deal with other players, and be mentally tough enough to not worry about circumstances that you cannot control, such as the type of field you play on, the officiating, or the weather.

The pyramid is a great visual aid to consider when choosing what areas to focus on next as a soccer player, coach, or parent. However, remember that a team's pyramid may look slightly different based on which tactics the players can handle and which approach the coach decides to use for games. Now that you know where this book plays into the bigger picture, let us begin.

Remember that if there are any words or terms whose meaning you are unsure of; you can feel free to reference the glossary at the back of the book.

Finally, if you enjoy this book, please leave a review on Amazon letting me know.

Chapter 1

Shooting a Driven Shot

Any action in soccer can be broken down into its essential components. The four guidelines of a driven shot to ensure precision, accuracy, and power are:

1. Start diagonal to the ball.
2. Plant a foot away from the ball.
3. On the foot you are striking the ball with, have your toe down and out with your knee facing the target so that you can use the bone of your foot.
4. Follow through, land on your shooting foot, bring your back leg forward, and point your hips where you want the ball to go.

1. **Stand at a 45° angle "diagonal" to the ball.** You want to be three or four steps from the ball to begin a running start to the ball because the faster you move towards the ball; the more power your shot will naturally have once you make contact. Comparatively, standing still and trying to strike the ball will reduce the power in your shot. As you stand at a 45° diagonal angle to the ball, your shoulders should be facing the ball as you

approach it. Being directly behind the ball when you approach it will result in the following: (1) Your shot will be diagonal across the goal's frame, which will result in a missed shot; and (2) You will have to change the part of your foot that you strike the ball with to have an accurate shot. Therefore, it will not be a driven shot. It will either be a shot with the inside of your foot (i.e., a pass shot) or a toe ball/toe blow/toe poke.

2. **Run at the ball and plant with the non-striking leg one foot away from the ball**. The taller you are, the further you plant away. The smaller you are, the closer you plant to the ball, but for the average person, you will be planting about a foot away. Planting too close to the ball will make it so that you have to change the part of the foot that you are using to strike the ball. Therefore, it will no longer be a driven shot, which is also known as a sledgehammer shot. Plant too far away from the ball and you will barely be able to reach the ball and will lose nearly all of the power on your shot. Make sure your plant foot is pointing at the portion of the net that you are looking to place the ball with your shot.

3. Fully contract your leg back to bring your foot behind your body. Bending at the knee and the hip allows you to bring your foot back correctly. **If you only bend at the knee or the hip, you will lose a lot of muscle on the shot and therefore a lot of power.** Bending at the knee allows your quadriceps to be engaged when striking the ball. Bending at the hip allows your hip flexor to be involved in the shot. Put them together and you will have a much harder shot. As you begin to drive your leg through the ball for a shot forcibly, make sure that your toe is down and out, and your knee is facing the target. Keep in mind that the target is not the net.

The target is where the goalkeeper is not in the net. Therefore, do not only point your knee at the net. First, determine the portion of the net that you want to strike the ball towards. Turn your knee so that it is facing outward instead of facing the target; this will allow you to shoot the ball with the inside of your foot. For many soccer players, this tends to be more accurate because it is very close to the form of passing. However, because the inside of your foot is softer than the hardest portion of your foot—which you normally use when you strike the ball with your toe down and out—your shot will lose a lot of power.

If you practice exclusively with your toe facing down and out, taking inside of the foot shots will not be comfortable. Being most comfortable with driven shots is for the best because the inside of the foot shots are not nearly as powerful and much easier to defend by a goalkeeper versus a driven shot if they are both placed in the same spot on the net. **As your leg follows through the ball, use the bone of your foot (i.e., the hardest portion of your foot where the laces meet the leather towards the inside of your foot) to strike the ball.** If you are looking for more power on your shot, striking the ball with the hardest portion of your foot will ensure there is power.

Think of the bone of your foot almost as if it is a baseball "bat," whereas further along your foot (i.e., towards your toes) is more like a "broom." A "bat" is harder than a "broom," so using the "bat" to hit the ball will give you more power than using the "broom." However, there is a time to use both portions of the top of your foot. If you are trying to loft the ball over a wall or a defender, striking the ball with the bone/"bat" of your foot will likely send it flying over the net or over the person, which you are trying to loft the ball too. Striking the ball towards the top of your toes (i.e., the "broom") will allow the ball to go over the wall or defender, but then dip down because it will not have as much power.

4. After striking the ball, follow through with your leg to generate more power and accuracy in your shot. Follow through with your opposite leg as well. **After you strike the ball, land past the spot on the field where you struck the ball initially.** Essentially, you must strike the ball and follow through to a spot past where you kicked it. Following through is similar to throwing a punch. You would not throw the punch with just your arm; you would use your entire body—including your hips—to turn at the waist and extend your arm as you throw the punch to generate more power. Similarly, you generate power for nearly all athletic moves with your hips.

Similarly, you do not want to strike the ball with just your leg. You want to strike it using your leg and your entire body. The bone/"bat" of your foot is the portion that makes contact with the ball. Then, you will follow through your shot, land past the ball, and bring your planting leg forward while pointing your hips at your target. Again, the target is the portion of the net where the goalkeeper is not located. Bringing your back leg/planting leg forward is key to easily allow you to turn your hips towards the portion of the net you want the ball to travel. Learn more about how to score in the *Understand Soccer* series book, *Soccer Shooting & Finishing: A Step-by-Step Guide on How to Score.*

Tip: Visualizing your shot (or anything you will do in soccer or in life) before you take it is about 70-80% as effective as actually having taken a practice shot from that same spot.

Tip: Keeping your head down while you strike the ball keeps your chest over the ball, keeps your form together for a more accurate shot, and reduces the chance that the ball will go flying over the net. Personally, I know it is tough to keep your head down. I like to watch all my shots go in as well. **However, lifting your head will worsen your form**. Would you rather view all your goals and have less of them or be the top scorer on the team, but only see a few of your goals?

Chapter 2

Finishing

Although the first chapter was on shooting, this chapter is about making sure you do not shoot just to shoot. It will help you learn how to ensure that your shots result in goals for your team. In the previous chapter, we went over how to strike a ball using the bone of your foot, so that you can make a driven and powerful shot. Now, we will discuss tactics to increase the probability of your well-driven shot going in the net. **To be a good finisher, you must aggressively push the ball, and then explode away with the ball after completing a skill.** There are three essential reasons for this:

1. **It provides space between you and the defender.** Therefore, you will have slightly more time to pick your head up to see where the goalkeeper is not to aim your shot.

2. **If you accelerate after pushing the ball, you will have more speed while running to the ball, which will result in a more powerful shot.** For example, imagine you are standing still, and you strike a shot with your foot planted next to the ball. You can kick it a lot farther with a run-up because your momentum, your body, and your hips can help you strike through the ball.

3. **An aggressive push past the defender gets you closer to the net.** The closer you are to the net, the more accurate you will be as the net becomes bigger. Additionally, because you are closer to the net, the goalkeeper is going to have less time to react and stop your shot.

Pushing the ball past a defender is best suited for when you have

just performed a foot skill. Push the ball with the outside portion of your laces about 5-7 yards behind the defender. Please keep in mind that faster players can afford to push the ball farther than slower players. Also, a 5 to 7-yard push works great when you are going against only one defender, but if there is another defender behind the one you just used a foot skill on, then you should use a smaller push that will travel 2-3 yards. This will help avoid pushing the ball into the supporting defender's feet.

It is critical that you go into a game with the mindset that you will be taking shots. **If your current mindset has you a little bit scared to shoot, you are likely not going to be a good finisher.** You have to have confidence in yourself, so as you read this book and implement the skills, tips, and tricks this book mentions, you will gain confidence in your striking and will consider yourself a finisher. You do not always have to hit the ball with the bone of your foot for it to be a good shot. When you watch professional players, they will use a driven shot, a shot with passing form, a toe-poke, and even use the outside of their foot.

Using all portions of your foot will help trick your defenders. **Toe-pokes allow you to have a lot of power with very little leg motion.** By just extending your knee and hitting the ball with your toe, most defenders are not prepared for an attacker to kick the ball with his or her toe. Most players have been trained from a very young age that kicking a ball with their toe is not a proper way to kick the ball. However, if you watch Ronaldo and Ronaldinho, you will notice they use a toe-poke on occasion because it brings an element of surprise. Also, you will even find soccer players using the outside of their foot to strike the ball. Shooting with the outside of your foot is a more technical way to fire a shot, but also **brings an element of surprise as most**

defenders do not expect you to strike a ball using the outside laces of your shooting foot.

Furthermore, you do not have to be entirely past the defender to take a shot. **All you need is just a little bit of space to create a shot that is effective and on target.** If the defender has been covering you well during the game, then shooting into their shins/ankles is not going to help your team at all, but keep in mind that you miss 100% of the shots you do not take. It is much more important for a soccer team to increase the volume of its shots because taking more shots results in more chances for the ball to go in.

Let us play out a situation; a team that takes 30 shots in a game versus a team that takes five really good shots. The team that takes 30 shots is still probably going to win because there are more opportunities for the goalkeeper to accidentally make a mistake, for the shooting team to have a lucky shot, or for the goalkeeper to give up a rebound and a teammate places the rebound into the back of the net.

Tip: Make sure to emphasize that shooting the ball over the net is absolutely unacceptable. **A shot over the net is a waste of a chance.** Yes, the glamour goals (e.g., the ESPN Top 10 highlight plays) are generally the shots that go perfectly upper-90 past the goalkeeper. However, in reality, unless you are taking a free kick, those are very low probability shots.

You want to be striking high probability shots that increase your team's ability to score and these are shots that are low or on the ground. Frequently, the shots will be towards the far post. These are great because it is difficult for the goalkeeper to travel to the ground to stop a shot that is low to the ground. If he or she can reach the ball, usually there will be a rebound that ends up in the middle of the 18-yard box. As long as your team has someone positioned to find rebounds, they will be shooting on a mostly empty net. Shooting the ball over the net wastes your team's opportunity to score. It is not about taking more shots; it is about taking more shots on target.

Coaching Tip: It is important to realize that taking **shots from 35 yards out has a very low probability of those shots going in**. If your team has 30 shots in a game, and they are all from 35 yards out, then there is a pretty good chance you are not going to score a single one. Make sure your shots are reasonable. Do not be afraid to take a lot of shots at the top of the 18-yard box. It will ensure that you have many opportunities to score—or at least create a rebound, which another teammate can place in the net.

Chapter 3

Being Coachable

As an athlete, you must make sure that you are approachable and coachable. Having the ability to be coached ensures that you will absorb the knowledge your coaches give you. We like to think that we know everything, but being open to other people's opinions, ideas, and words of wisdom makes us even more knowledgeable Being coachable will enable you to learn more than another athlete who has a fixed mindset. **In sports and in life, it is critical to have a growth mindset and continually seek out new information.** This will help you learn new skills, tips, and tricks in all the endeavors you love. Not only is this important on the field; it is important in the classroom and at home.

Michael Jordan, the famous basketball player, was referenced by other players and coaches as being the most coachable player that they have ever played with or coached. Michael Jordan sought out other star players and great coaches to find ways to improve his game. He was willing to listen to everyone to find little nuggets and tidbits of information that were useful that he adopted to improve his game. He used the knowledge and a second-to-none work ethic to become one of the best basketball players of all time. However, keep in mind that even though **everyone may have an opinion, not everyone is worth listening to or qualified to give advice.** Have an initial conversation with that person or coach to see if they are someone from which you should be learning. Some people want to put in their "two cents," but it is not worth anything more than that.

Also, remember that learning only to learn will make you a fool. You must *apply* what you have learned. You have to take action! You will learn just as much from doing as you will from reading a book or listening to a coach. **If you never apply your knowledge, then you may understand it, but you will not *know* it until you can apply it consistently.**

Therefore, in a practice or a game, anytime the coach gives a piece of information to the entire group or you specifically, **make sure to thank them for the feedback even if they are doing it in a mean way.** If you want the coach to know that you are coachable because you care so much about being a better player, take action on what they say immediately. This mindset of immediate action will be very obvious to coaches and show them that you are open to their feedback. Also, remember that it is just feedback, not a personal attack against you. It is not that they hate you, are trying to tear you down, or want to make you less of a player; it is instead that they care about you and want you to improve rapidly. If you show that you care about their opinions and implement their teachings, they will like you even more. As a result, they will play you even more and you will learn the most possible from them.

Parenting Tip: Use the sandwich technique when giving feedback. First, give your child compliment on something they are performing well. Keep the praise quick and straightforward, such as, "Good job approaching the ball diagonally." Then, give constructive feedback and explain why it is important. For example, say, "Plant your foot farther from the ball; this will allow you to turn your toe down and out more." Finally, end with another compliment and explanation, such as, "Great job following through; it will ensure you have plenty of power on your shot."

This sandwich method is crucial for helping players that have a fixed mindset. By beginning with a compliment, you will break down any walls they have built up against feedback. By ending with a compliment, you leave them with a good feeling that they are doing most things correctly. By providing feedback in the middle of two compliments, you make sure that they hear your message and that they have positive associations with it. Include explanations for all three to guarantee that your message sticks.

Coaching Tip: Make sure that anytime you give advice, do not attack the player; just address the situation. Addressing the situation is critical because if one of your players does something counterproductive, it has nothing to do with who they are as a person. Therefore, correct what they did but avoid offending them personally.

What often works for me is to let them know:

1.How I have made the same types of mistakes
2.Exactly what I did wrong
3.What I did to correct it
4.The outcome of the changes I made

For example, I often ask my trainees, "How old do you think I was when I first learned to use my left foot?" I let them guess until they find out I was 14 years old. Then, I ask them if that is good or bad. They tell me it is bad, and I agree with them. Then, I let them know that I make mistakes too, but because I learned that it is essential to use both feet, I practiced using my left foot for an entire summer. I used it exclusively until I was proficient, and it was helpful instead of holding me back.

Now, because I am better dribbling with my right foot than with my left foot, so the ball ends up on my left foot after I perform a foot skill. Therefore, I score more goals with my left foot than my right foot, and I score more goals overall because I can effectively use both feet, which causes the defender to have a difficult time trying to prevent me from scoring. This is all because I took massive action and practiced improving one of my weaknesses. If you are a coach and want more information on the most important things for a coach to focus on, then grab a copy of the *Understand Soccer* series book, *Soccer Coaching: A Step-by-Step Guide on How to Lead Your Players, Manage Parents, and Select the Best Formation.*

Chapter 4

Parenting

As the parent of a soccer player, it is vital that you are continually supportive of and reassuring to your child. **Only focusing on the bad aspects of their game and criticizing their performance will just drive them away from the game they love.** This is not to say that you should never give them any feedback on areas to improve; however, pick your battles. As they are still growing, they are also still working on developing their self-confidence.

Constant criticisms will only tear them down and will not build them up in the way that is productive. Some easy things to do are celebrate their successes if they score a goal, make an assist, or help the team achieve their goal of winning a game. **Tell him or her "good job," give him or her a pat on the back, and brag about him or her in front of other people.** However, in situations where they do not do so good, still be supportive of them.

As mentioned previously in the book, use the sandwich technique where you compliment them for something that they are doing well. Give them some feedback on something you noticed that they could improve, but make sure that it indeed is something that must be improved. Frequently, parents will think that their kid is supposed to be doing one thing on the field, whereas the coach has them doing something entirely different. Make sure your communication lines are open as a parent working with your child to help them become a better player. **Having a good relationship and excellent communication with your child will ensure that they bring things up to you.**

For example, my sister played center midfield. Growing up, she started her soccer career in the American Youth Soccer Organization (AYSO). At a younger age than many of her soccer peers, she began using much larger nets, so she had much more experience striking shots that were higher in the air. The nets were a lot bigger, and the goalkeepers could not reach most of the spots farther up in the net. In fact, she averaged over a goal a game, and nearly all of them were shots that went over the goalkeeper's head and outreached arms. However, after a disappointing loss, her travel soccer coach told the entire team that he did not want anyone shooting from outside the 18-yard box.

For the next several games, my sister no longer shot from the spots where she scored nearly all of her goals. Therefore, my parents asked her why she was not shooting as she previously had done when she was outside of the 18-yard box. She mentioned to them that the coach told everyone to stop shooting from that far out, so she no longer did it because she wanted to follow the coach's direction.

Then, my parents, who were upset by this information because it was making it so that she was not scoring from the spots that she usually scored from, decided to approach the coach and nicely asked him why he said that to the team. He said "oh my gosh, she is following that advice? I meant that for the other girls on the team because they were trying to shoot the ball like her. All of their shots were going right to the goalkeeper, were not powerful, and not above the goalkeeper to score."

Had my parents not had a good relationship with my sister or the ability to communicate what they noticed in a game; my sister would have stopped shooting from outside the 18-yard box for the rest of the season. They had many more games that season, and she would not have taken her usual shots. Therefore, it is critical that you keep the communication lines open with your child and avoid criticism in most circumstances.

Constructive criticism wrapped in compliments works very well. **Rewarding the good produces more good, whereas criticizing the bad often produces more bad.** Focus on what you want and for the most part, let the bad fall by the wayside. If you want to learn more, grab a copy of the *Understand Soccer* series book, *Soccer Parenting: A Step-by-Step Guide on How to Build Your Child's Confidence, Work with the Coach, and Help Your Soccer Player Succeed.*

Parenting Tip: Be reasonable with coaches. **Be honest with yourself.** If your child is not the best player on the team, then mentally acknowledge it and seek to improve their skills by increasing their understanding of the game and potentially adding additional training. The coach is likely doing their best with all the information they have. Keep in mind that although we wish this were not the case, the worse your relationship with the coach is, the more it will affect your child's positioning and play time. Just as you give your child compliments, keep in mind that coaches love to hear praise for what they are doing well too. If you are interested in learning about the 20+ different positions your child can play on the field, then grab a copy of the *Understand Soccer* series book, *Soccer Positions: A Step-by-Step Guide About Each Player on a Team.*

Coaching Tip: As a coach, sometimes you have to deal with unruly parents. Many of us have had parents that thought their kid was an absolute all-star. However, we both know that they probably should not have even come off the bench with their subpar performances. That same parent will be personally offended when you do not play their son or daughter as much as they think is appropriate. **Here, one of the worst things you can do is to tell them that their kid is not good.** You want to be gentle and explain that as a coach, you are trying to have the team to work as well as possible. Mention that their performance has been lacking a little bit in practices, so you reward good results in practices with playing time in games. This statement does multiple things:

1. It lets parents know that their kid will play if they improve.

2. It gently lets them know that their kid has room for improvement, which can be achieved via additional training, courses, and books.

3. It keeps you from appearing to be the enemy and reinforces that you just want the best result for the team. Remember that if one parent dislikes you, and they have some influence with the other parents, then the problem could snowball, and many parents may turn against you, which will destroy the team's chemistry. Above all, remember that this is still your team. You are the coach, and you may make some mistakes. You are human, and mistakes can happen in a game.

Perhaps you played someone in an incorrect position versus what would have been better for the team, but you just did not know it at the time. **Therefore, keep in mind that mistakes will occur, but errors should be viewed only as feedback.** Remind yourself that they are just parents letting you know that they are distraught or that they feel something was wrong and it should be improved upon going forward. Be open to the feedback. Do not see the parents as the enemy. See their opinions as opportunities to grow. Improve your ability to communicate as a coach and learn from other people's perspectives because when you watch the game, you only have one set of eyes to view the action.

Parents may see other things that you cannot fully view. If they bring their perspectives to you, **say "Thank you for the feedback,"** and tell them you will surely consider what they said. This ensures that they will be on your side and looking out for your best interest. Keep the communication lines open with parents so that they will want their child to be on your team. This will lessen the amount of parents who are distraught over their child's play time, position, etc.

Chapter 5

Foot Skills

Though there are many skills for a soccer player to develop, having effective foot skills will get you past defenders will build your self-confidence like nothing else. The four essential foot skills are as follows:

1. Body Feint (i.e., a "feint, "fake," "fake and take," "jab step," or "shoulder drop")
2. Self-Pass (i.e., an "L," "la croqueta, " or "Iniesta")
3. Shot Fake
4. Cut

When performing foot skills, it is vital to remember that you are trying to be as quick and as efficient as possible. Whether you like him or not, Lionel Messi is arguably the best dribbler in the world. If you ever watch Lionel Messi play, he does not use very flashy moves such as the scissor, rolls, rainbows, etc. Messi uses skills that enable him to be as quick as possible to travel past the defenders.

Quite honestly, when you watch him, it does not even look like he is using that many skills at all. It seems like he is just running around people on the other team. When you make it look like you are just running past defenders, it is a sign of excellent foot skills. The more in-depth a move is, the more time it takes. **The more time a skill takes, the easier it is for the defender to recover and steal the ball from you or for support to help the defender out in taking the ball from you.**

1. **A "body feint" or a "jab step" is when you pretend to push the**

ball in one direction past the defender. However, you purposely miss the ball, then plant with the foot that you just missed the ball with, at which point you push the ball in the other direction past the defender. It is critically important to make sure to sell this move with your shoulders and hips. This means that you should not only miss the ball with the leg that pretended to push the ball, but also to have your hips and shoulders pointing in the direction you are trying to fake the defender into believing you are traveling.

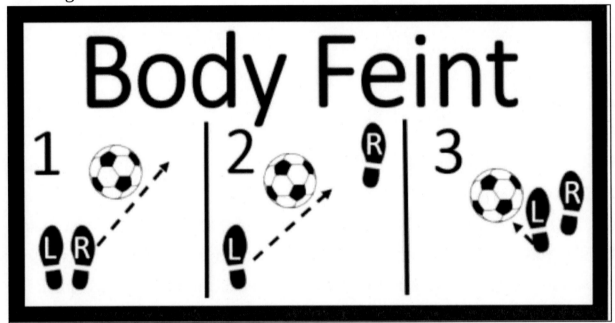

  Use this skill when you are attacking, and the defender is backpedaling (i.e., jockeying) you. All you are trying to do in this instance is get the defender to plant a little bit too firmly on one leg because of your foot skill. If they plant too heavily with one leg, they cannot reach very far when you explode past them in the other direction. Two things that seemingly overnight had changed my ability to attack a defender was the knowledge of:

  You do not have to be directly behind the defender to beat the defender. If you are close enough to the net and you create just enough space to shoot, then the skill is considered successful, granted you are taking a decent shot or making a quality pass.

A skill buys you a little bit of time. A move done correctly results in the defender planting too heavily on one leg or a bit of a flinch from the defender. **However, the real way that you create space with your skill is the acceleration after the skill.** When you watch the likes of Lionel Messi, Neymar, Ronaldo, you notice that after any skill they perform, they explode with speed to run away from the defender.

2. The self-pass, also known as the Iniesta, is nicknamed after the famous Barcelona midfielder and captain Andrés Iniesta. Furthermore, he helped lead the Spanish national team to Euro Cup and World Cup wins. It is nicknamed after him because he uses it so frequently and more than any other player. **The self-pass is simply just a pass from one foot to the other while you are running with the ball.** Imagine you are doing a roll (i.e., a rollover), but without your foot going on top of the ball. Instead, the self-pass is an inside of the foot pass with one foot and an inside of the foot push up the field with the other foot. The motion that the ball makes is that of the letter "L" or a reversed "L." The self-pass will help you travel directly behind the defender, but if you open up the foot that is pushing the ball up the field, you will be able to push the ball diagonal to your body, which will set you up for a driven shot on net.

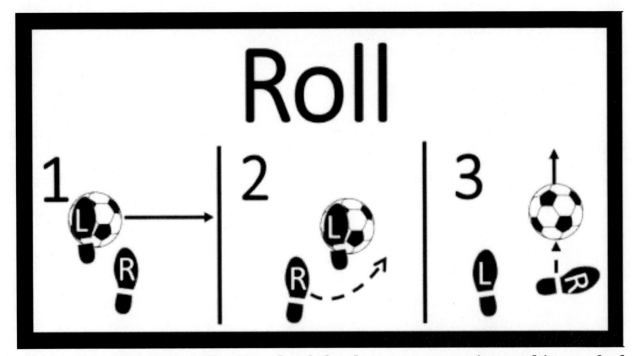

Use this foot skill when the defender over-commits, and instead of jockeying you, they jump in to steal the ball. Since they are lunging towards you and the ball, their momentum is going in the opposite direction that you are travelling. Therefore, all you need to do is move the ball away from their incoming foot and push it forward with the foot that received the pass from the other foot. Being explosive after the skill helps, but not nearly as much as it does for a feint because all the defender's momentum is going in the opposite direction you are going.

As a result, once the defender misses the ball when they have jumped in, they will have to completely come to a stop and then start sprinting at full speed again back towards the direction they came. **To go from a full sprint to a stop back to a full sprint takes a considerable amount of time.** For many players, this move is not as easy to master initially as a roll would be, however, it is much faster and more efficient of a skill when you have it mastered.

YouTube: If you would like to see how to perform a self-pass in a video format, consider watching the *Understand Soccer* YouTube video: *La Croqueta - How to Self-Pass*.

3. A "shot fake" is when you fake a shot. Similarly, you can do a pass fake when you pretend to make a pass. These are used anywhere on the field, but as you travel closer to the net, what would have typically been a pass fake, now is more likely to be a shot fake. As you travel closer to the goal, the other team understands your objective is to shoot and to score. **Shot fakes**

are very helpful at making the defender flinch/freeze for half a second so that you can change your direction and accelerate away with speed. Shot fakes are great whether the defender is close to you or far away.

When the defender is several yards away from you, they will flinch because they do not want to be hit with the ball when you pretend to shoot it. If they are very close to you when you do a shot fake, they will overreach thinking that you will shoot the ball. They will reach out to stop the "shot," which allows you to cut the ball and change your direction while accelerating away. **To do a shot fake correctly, you must make it look exactly like a shot.** That means the shooting leg must go all the way back and your arms go up exactly the same way as if you were going to shoot the ball.

Most players do not lift their head slightly before they do a shot fake. In most game situations, a good striker is going to make sure they know where the goalkeeper is before they shoot the ball. If the goalkeeper has poor positioning in the net, they will shoot it where the goalkeeper is not in the net. If the goalkeeper has proper positioning, then a great striker will shoot where the goalkeeper is not (often to the far post).

Shooting to the part of the net where the goalkeeper is not located means that the striker must shoot a more tactical and challenging shot on net. However, because you are doing a shot fake, the defender will notice if you did not lift your head for a glance. **They will realize that your shot fakes differ from your real shots and they will have more success defending against you because you did not make your shot and your shot fake look the same.**

YouTube: If you would like to see when to use each shot fake in a video format, then consider watching the *Understand Soccer* YouTube video: *Fake Shot - Which Shot Fake to Use*.

YouTube: If you would like to see all the Tier 1 and Tier 2 shot fakes performed in a video format, then consider watching the *Understand Soccer* YouTube video: *How To Fake Shot In Soccer*.

4. A "Cut" is used to change directions. Add a shot fake to this skill and it makes for a great skill to change your direction while giving you space. **A cut is simply stopping the ball with the inside or outside of your foot and then pushing the ball in a direction that is different than the direction you were previously dribbling.** To correctly perform a cut (i.e., a chop) with the outside of your foot, your leg that is cutting the ball must step entirely past the ball. Then, allow the ball to hit your foot, which effectively stops the ball.

Since the ball is on the outside of your foot, the outside of the foot cut is perfect to accelerate away because the ball is perfectly where you would need it to be to push it using your laces with your toe down and in. **An inside of the foot cut is often better used when you are along a sideline pretending to cross the ball and you cut the ball to keep it in front of you to attack in a different direction.**

Tip: A "scissor" is not the same thing as a step-over. **A step-over is when you are next to the ball, and your farthest leg from the ball steps over the ball. Then, your entire body turns as though you are going one way, but you miss the ball so that you can accelerate in the opposite direction.** A scissor is when your foot closest to the ball goes around the ball as you attack. A step-over is excellent to use along the sidelines whereas it is best to use the scissor (similar to a feint) when attacking a defender that is backpedaling/jockeying you.

YouTube: If you would like to see how to perform a step-over in a video format, then consider watching the *Understand Soccer* YouTube video: *Step-Over - How To*.

Tip: Many players train and practice the scissor. The scissor is okay at best, but it requires an extra step to plant in front of the ball. An additional step allows the player to be past the ball enough so that when you pretend to push it in one direction past the defender, the ball can roll between your legs and you can accelerate in the other direction.

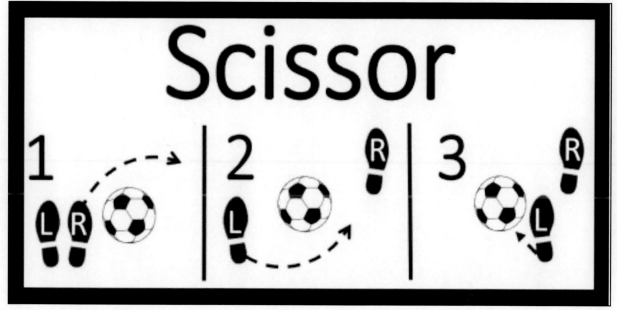

Most people teach the scissor in a way that makes it look like a "magic wand." Imagine a magic show you have seen on television, in movies, or in real life. The magician waves their wand over their hat. That is what most players' scissor looks like because they throw their leg over the ball, but they do not actually go around the ball. Also, they never turn their hips, so the defender is infrequently faked out by the foot skill. **The scissor is okay to practice if you have the body feint down perfectly, but the feint is more efficient than the scissor.**

Chapter 6

Dribbling

The ability to dribble a ball is essential to be productive on the field. There are several points to consider to dribble correctly and ensure your success on the soccer field:

1. Keep the toe of your dribbling foot down and in
2. Less touches will allow you to dribble faster
3. Use less touches when you have more space
4. Raise your head slightly
5. Practice dribbling with both feet

1. Have your toe down and in on the foot that is pushing the ball, which places you on the balls of your feet (e.g., point A in the picture). When a coach tells you to run on your toes, they are really saying to run on your toes and the balls of your feet. Likewise, anytime you go on your "tippy-toes," you are really on your toes and the balls of your feet. Having your toes "down and in" on the foot that is pushing the ball will make a cupping shape (similar to an ice cream scooper) with your foot that allows the ball to fit perfectly on your laces as you push it with each step. Notice that it is "toe down and in." Note that you must turn your foot slightly inside so that you can effectively push the ball with your laces. Otherwise, you will only poke it forward, and you cannot run with much speed if your toe is down but not in. You will end up hitting the ground way too often with your toes, which will slow you down.

2. Something that dramatically changed my speed of play overnight was when I realized that **the more space you have, the fewer touches you should take**. The more touches you take, the more time it takes to travel the

same distance. Taking unnecessary touches allows the defender more time to close you down and steal the ball, and it allows players on the opposing team more time to hustle back and help stop you. This concept is counter-intuitive for most players, as they think more touches means better skill, which will result in being a better soccer player. However, in a recent college soccer player training class I conducted, I noticed that many of the college players took two or three more touches to cover space that could have easily been done in one.

3. The closer the person defending is to you, the smaller the touches you will want to take, except when you take your explosive touch after a skill to push away from the defender. **Also, if you are dribbling in a congested portion of the field, such as the central midfield area, you will generally take smaller touches.** The center midfielders have defenders, outside midfielder, and forwards creeping into their space. Let us not forget they also likely have another center midfielder on their team and two from the opposing team to consider in their area too.

In these instances, because there are so many people around a center midfielder, they generally will and should take smaller touches than an outside midfielder, forward, or outside defender. Smaller touches will allow a center midfielder to be in closer contact with the ball. Therefore, they can quickly push and dribble the ball away from an opposing team player's foot. **However, as a forward with more space and an outside midfielder who has a ton of room on the soccer field, taking bigger touches allows you to have an explosive attack and a very good counterattack when your team steals possession of the ball.**

4. An important point to keep in mind when dribbling is that you want your head raised a bit so that you are looking about 5 yards in front of you while you dribble. Looking ahead of you makes it so you can still see the ball in your peripheral vision, but can also now see the defenders and other teammates' positioning on the field. Being a good dribbler is as much about being able to take good touches as it is being able to pick your head up to see if there is a better option on the field for you than for you to keep dribbling.

Let us face it; we have all played with someone who is exceptionally good at dribbling and quite entertaining to watch but keeps their head down the entire time. Though they may do some productive things with the ball, they are not doing nearly much as a player who picks their head up a little bit. The other team is going to recognize when someone keeps their head down while they dribble, and so they will apply more pressure on them and because they do not look up to see where their teammates are located on the field. **These players are not very fun to play with because they hardly pass the ball to anyone.**

5. Naturally, dribbling with both feet is very important. **In fact, dribbling with your opposite foot instead of your dominant foot will make you a better soccer player.** Many of the skills you use to beat a defender require that you fake to take it with your opposite foot. Then, you can push and take it with your dominant foot to either continue dribbling or take a shot. Having a strong opposite foot was something I did not realize was necessary for the longest time. I would do a lot of dribbling with my dominant right foot, which would then put me on my left foot for a shot. I compensated so much for it that I probably took twice as many shots with my

opposite foot as I did with my dominant foot. Had I developed a stronger opposite foot; it would have resulted in more shots taken with my dominant foot.

Keep in mind that in most game situations, a good defender will push you on to your opposite foot. As a result, I scored more goals with my left foot, since I took more shots with my left foot because I was a slightly better dribbler with my right foot. Avoid this as much as possible and learn to be a good dribbler with your opposite foot so that, after a skill, the ball will be on your dominant foot when you go to shoot. After all, dribbling is what you do to place the ball where you want it, whether you are looking to shoot the ball or make a pass. If you cannot dribble well, you are not going to have many opportunities to pass or shoot the ball. To learn the most important skills; pick up a copy of the *Understand Soccer* series book, *Soccer Dribbling & Foot Skills: A Step-by-Step Guide on How to Dribble Past the Other Team.*

Tip: When dribbling, slowing yourself down reduces your momentum tremendously. Slowing down decreases your ability to make progress on the field, which makes it very easy for the other team to catch up with you. Ideally, when dribbling, remain at as high of a speed as possible to avoid more of the opposing team's defenders and midfielders hustling back to provide support and take the ball. However, please keep in mind that running faster while you dribble will slightly increase your chances of making a mistake. Avoiding mistakes at your top speed is one of the many reasons why it is so important to practice at game speed.

Coaching Tip: An excellent way to start a practice is with fast footwork to work on dribbling. Yes, even for high school and college-level players, focusing on making sure that they are taking a touch with their toe down and in and having their head raised is more important than many of the skills that can be used while you dribble. When you practice dribbling, vary it between speed dribbling and taking small touches. **Speed dribbling is when you take a touch every single step, but your step is a very long stride.** Also, include small touch dribbling to develop their habit of having their toe down and in. It allows you to take a lot more touches in the same amount of space because you are not using as long of a stride. When practicing taking small touches, you are really going for a large quantity of touches.

YouTube: If you would like to see how to dribble effectively in a video format, then consider watching the *Understand Soccer* YouTube video: *Dribbling in Soccer Technique*.

Chapter 7

Defending

As a defender, your body positioning should be angled. Your hips should never be completely pointed (i.e., "squared") at the attacker because the attacker can go to your right, left, or between your legs. **You should be angled but not entirely turned to the side.** Position one side of your body so that it is facing the attacker but is still diagonal. If your feet were hands on a clock, they should be positioned at "10 and 4," as shown in the first image, or "8 and 2," as shown in the second image.

This body positioning will allow you to push the attacker either to the left or the right. Standing at "10 and 4" will push them to their left foot and standing at "8 and 2" will push them to their right foot. Keep in mind that just standing directly in front of them and turning your hips will not force them in the direction you want them to go. **You must be slightly off-centered, with your hips set at either "10 and 4" or "8 and 2" to push them in the direction that you want them to go.** If you just turn your hips directly in front of a good dribbler, then they will attack the side you are not facing to make it easier for themselves.

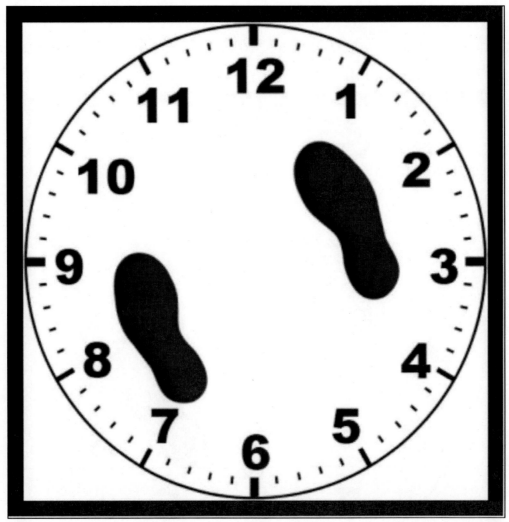

   As a defender, it is essential to remain active on your toes. You do not want to stand still. You want to bend at the knees and hips while being lower in your stance. This will allow you to accelerate faster when the attacker does a skill and attempts to sprint away.

Nearly all trainees do not realize is that they need to make themselves bigger. The most straightforward and easiest way to do that is to pick your arms up. From a young age, players are often taught to keep your arms by their sides. **However, in a game, 19 out of 20 times, the referee is not going to call you if your arms are up.** If you ever watch professional defenders, they tend to use their hands and arms a lot because, in most situations, the referee is not going to call anything against them. Therefore, you should not worry about keeping your arms down. Instead, extend your elbow and shoulder to engage with them. It is crucial that you make yourself look bigger than you are for a few reasons:

1. It will naturally cause an attacker's confidence to decrease.

2. It will be harder for them to travel around you because you can more quickly use your arm to generate momentum as you turn.

3. Having your arms up makes it easier to place your forearm against their body and use your shoulder muscle to keep them away from the ball.

If you would like more information on how to defend in 1v1s, 2v1s, 1v2s, 2v2s, and to learn exactly where to push the defender, then grab a copy of the *Understand Soccer* series book, *Soccer Defending: A Step-by-Step Guide on How to Stop the Other Team.*

Tip: In a 1v1 game situation, where you push the defender depends on the portion of the field they are on and their location relative to your teammates. Ideally, if you are in the middle of the field, you would want to push the attacker to their weak foot. How do you know which foot is there weak foot? **Always assume it is their left foot until they prove you otherwise.** However, when you are along a sideline and it is still a one versus one, you want to position your body in a way that will push them towards the sideline and out of bounds.

Tip: If another defender is supporting you, then a good attacker will take a route that requires them to beat only one defender. **However, a good defender will push the attacker into their partner** to increase the chance that one of them can take the ball away. This is because two players' feet reaching for the ball will likely be a lot better than just one.

YouTube: If you would like to see how to position your body as a defender in a video format, then consider watching the *Understand Soccer* YouTube video: *Defending Skills - Body Positioning.*

Chapter 8

Passing the Ball

As a soccer player, it is important to have the fundamentals down when passing. You can pass the ball with different parts of your foot, but your most frequently used passing form is with the inside of your foot, as follows:

1. Plant next to the ball while pointing your foot and hips at your partner
2. Toe up, heel down, and ankle locked
3. Knees slightly bent and foot slightly off the ground
4. Follow through after making contact with the ball

1. The form for a pass and a shot are different. **With passing form,**

you should plant much closer to the ball because your body mechanics will allow you to turn your leg and pass the ball with the inside of your foot. Similarly, point the foot that is planted on the ground at the person or the open space to which you are passing the ball. Your plant leg should be slightly bent, just like with shooting form. You definitely do not want a straight leg when you plant for a shot or a pass. Also, make sure to turn your hips towards the person or area of the field that you are passing the ball.

2. **Point your toe all the way up, which makes your heel go down.** Having your toe up and heal down naturally locks your ankle. Having a locked ankle will make it so that you have a powerful and more accurate pass. Also, locking your ankle allows the surface of your foot that you are passing the ball with (i.e., the side of your foot) to be wider. A wider foot creates less room for error so that if you miscalculate a little bit where the ball will be, you have a broader surface to ensure a more accurate pass. Conversely, if your toe is pointed down and your heel is up, your ankle will be loose, resulting in a lack of power on your pass. Also, you are making your foot smaller and narrower, which means that your pass will be inaccurate if misjudged even slightly for where the ball will be.

3. **Keep the knee from your passing leg slightly bent.** Your leg should not be straight, both when you are passing and in nearly all game instances. When you straighten your leg, and you stand straight, you are not engaging the strongest muscle group of your legs, which are your quadriceps. Therefore, you are not going to be as explosive when you shoot, pass, dribble, run, jump, etc. If you keep your leg bent, your foot will naturally be slightly off the ground. If you pass the ball with your foot touching or close to the ground, the pass will result in the ball popping up into the air. Part of

passing is to make sure that you are making it as easy as possible for your teammate. After all, soccer is a team sport, so if you consistently pass the ball in the air, you will make it more difficult for your teammates. They will likely then have to focus their first touch on trapping the ball on the ground, and their second touch on attacking in the space. Ideally, your pass should be firm, accurate, and on the ground so that their first touch can be into space on the field.

4. **Next, make sure you follow through on your pass.** What you do with your leg after you fully follow through depends on the situation that you are in during the game, scrimmage, or practice. Most times, after you make a pass, you will be running to another spot on the field to keep developing the play. Therefore, as you pass the ball (similar to a shot), you follow through and land on your passing foot. Then, you bring your back leg forward to take the next step. As you pass, you are already starting to continue to run and maintain your forward motion to the next spot on the field that you want to go. However, at times you will be passing the ball and you are not going to be a part of the attacking portion of that play. For example, players that may do this are a goalkeeper or in a few instances, a defender. Therefore, you follow through after you pass the ball, but then you bring your leg back to where it began the passing motion. As a result, you end up in the same spot you started when you are making this pass. If you would like more information on how to easily receive passes and pass around the other team so that you are confident every time you pass or receive a pass, the grab a copy of the *Understand Soccer* series book, *Soccer Passing & Receiving: A Step-by-Step Guide on How to Work with Your Teammates.*

Tip: Keeping your head down while you pass the ball keeps your chest over the ball and holds your form together for a more accurate pass. **Having your head over the ball reduces the chance that the ball will pop up into the air when you pass the ball.**

Tip: Keep most of your passes on the ground when playing to a teammate. However, if you are playing on a field of low quality that is bumpy in certain places, then consider passing slightly off the ground. If you pass on the ground, it will increase your chances of hitting a bumpy spot on the field, which will pop the ball into the air and slow its forward progress. By putting the ball in the air slightly off the ground, it will reduce the chances of hitting a rough spot and increase the probability that it is a good pass. Furthermore, make sure to pass the ball to a position that helps your teammate. **Generally, you should lead your teammate with a pass when there is no one in front of them.** In most circumstances, avoid passing behind your teammate because they must come to a complete stop and turn around to receive the pass if they are running up the field. However, this is appropriate when you are a defender passing to another defender on your team who has someone covering them.

YouTube: If you would like to see how to pass the ball effectively in a video format, then consider watching the *Understand Soccer* YouTube video: _How to Pass a Soccer Ball with the Inside of Your Foot_.

Chapter 9

Receiving the Ball

You can receive the ball with different parts of your foot, but the five general rules to receive a pass and ensure ball control and an accurate first touch are:

1. Plant next to the ball while pointing your foot and hips at your teammate
2. Toe up, heel down, and ankle locked
3. Knees slightly bent
4. Foot slightly off the ground
5. Typically, use the inside of the foot towards the heel to take a moving first touch

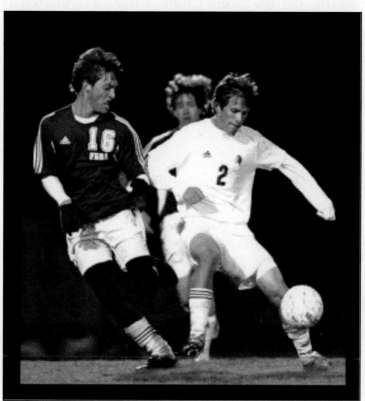

The form to receive a pass is the same as the first four steps of the form to make a pass. However, to receive a pass, there are a few more things to consider to make sure that you are productive with the ball:

1. **Demand the ball; do not ask for the ball. Yell for the ball; do not call for the ball.** These shifts in wording (i.e., "demand" versus "ask" and "yell" versus "call") do a few excellent things for you as the person who wants to receive a pass or be played a through ball.

Demanding the ball lets the person that is passing the ball know that you are very confident. It tells him or her that you will do something with the ball that is beneficial for your team. Think about it, if you are playing a game and have two people that you can pass the ball. The first person is screaming their head off demanding the ball. The other person is maybe showing for a pass, using a hand motion indicating that they want the ball, or meekly asking for the ball. Even if the person that is yelling for the ball is not quite as open, the player with the ball will consider passing it to them because they can hear it in their voice that they plan to do something with the ball. Also, demanding/yelling for the ball even if the person with the ball is close to you, ensures that he or she hears you.

Often, the person dribbling the ball is far away from you or potentially has a defender or two covering them. Therefore, by demanding/yelling for the ball, you let them know that you are open to receive the ball. **Many available passes in soccer are not made because the player with the ball did not know you were open.** They have their head down and looking at the ball, to protect the ball from the defender. Therefore, if they do not hear you with their ears, they are likely not going to see you with their eyes. Lastly, yelling for the ball builds confidence in yourself and increases your ability to help your team achieve its offensive objective of scoring!

2. **Depending on the situation in the game, you want to make sure that you check to the ball (i.e., go towards the ball) in most instances.** Now, you definitely do not want to do that when you are making a "through" run and you want them to play the pass in front of you. In these situations, you want to communicate (e.g., yell/hand motion/or start sprinting in a direction away from the play, but down the field) to them where you are going and let them pass the ball in front of you so that you can take your first touch in stride. More often than not, you will be receiving a pass and you should be checking to the ball to make sure that you successfully receive the ball.

It is frustrating for your coach and teammates when you are given a good pass and do not receive the ball because you are playing lazily. You must be active, on your toes, and stepping towards the pass to receive it. If you do not, it will allow the defender to come between you and the ball. This laziness will result in an intercepted pass. It will be very easy for the other team to start a counterattack if you lose possession during a simple pass.

3. **Before receiving a pass, make sure to scan the field and look behind you.** Having a good idea of what you plan to do before you actually do it will make you a much more effective and efficient soccer player, as well as a better teammate. It does not have to be a 5 to 10-second scan. It is just a quick swivel of the head to see if there is pressure and where some open teammates are for you to make a sensible pass or potentially dribble after you receive the ball. A quick look is something that sets college players apart from high school players and definitely professional players from college players.

These differences are things that coaches and scouts notice. An excellent defender, midfielder, or striker will assuredly know where teammates and opponents are on the field. Therefore, as they are receiving the pass, they are already thinking about what their next actions in the game will be. In soccer and life, if you fail to plan, you plan to fail. **By quickly scanning behind you, you are already starting to allow yourself mentally to have time to develop a plan of attack.** The fast scan will surely help you score more or deliver the pass that will allow your team to score.

4. **Next, when you receive a pass in most game situations, your hips should still be squared with your teammate.** Being squared with your teammate means pointing your hips at your teammate. When your hips are square with your teammate, your first touch will be more accurate. In this instance, you are creating an L with your stance by pointing your planted foot at your teammate. The foot you are receiving the pass with should be turned so that you can use the inside of your foot to take your first touch. This form is basically the same as the form you would use if you were making a pass.

5. **Roughly 95% of your first touches in a game should be moving first touches.** A moving touch pushes the ball into space with your first touch. A moving first touch is the opposite of taking a touch where the ball stops underneath you (i.e., at your feet). A moving first touch may go towards your opponent's net, towards your own net, or in any direction away from you. In a game, you should take moving first touches because it allows the ball to go in the direction that you want to take it while only using one touch.

More often than not, the moving first touch is into space on the field to give yourself more time to think, to pass, to dribble, to shoot, to do whatever you need to do with the ball. Next, by taking the first step with your moving touch, you will have a more accurate first touch. Looking at the picture, use part "B" to take a moving first touch with the hardest part of your foot, which can be referred to as the "bat."

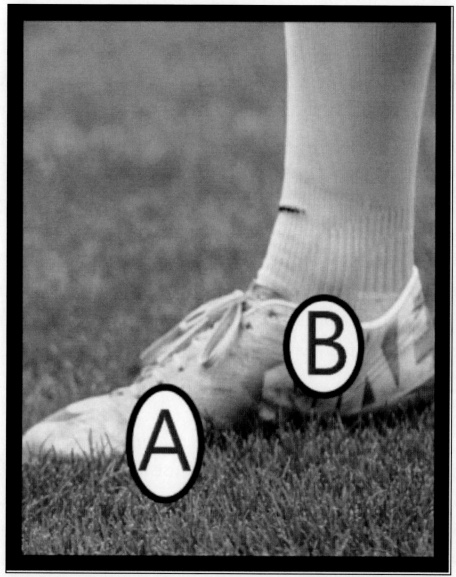

A moving first touch is not meant to push the ball really far away from you; it is intended for you to take your first step in the direction you want to go. **For the longest time, I did not realize that a moving first touch was key to being a fast soccer player.** I thought that you had to be a quick runner to be a fast soccer player. In reality, you have to be great with your first moving first touch to be a fast soccer player. This one tip alone changed my game overnight. The moving first touch helps your acceleration tremendously because you are already starting to build momentum and speed in the direction you want to go, which enables you to distance yourself from the defender who is marking you.

6. **Occasionally, it will be appropriate to take a touch underneath your body (i.e., a touch that stops at your feet).** This touch is necessary when you have too many people around you where someone could easily cut a moving first touch off and take possession of the ball from you. Only then is it okay to take your first touch under your body. Also, if you receive a difficult pass, ideally you still take an attacking first touch, but it is understandable if you take a first touch that stops underneath you and then you start attacking with the ball. Bad passes are generally ones played to you in the air. Looking at the picture again, use part "A" to take a touch with the softest portion of your foot, which can be referred to as the "broom" to settle the ball at your feet.

7. When you move to receive the pass, what you plan to do with the ball determines which portion of your foot to use to take a moving first touch. **Ideally, the moving first touch is really going to be a moving first step.** You are pushing the ball with the same portion of your foot (i.e., the inside of your ankle) that you pass a ball with because it should be locked and will push the ball better. However, if you are looking for the ball to stop underneath you, you will be taking your first touch with the inside of your foot up towards your toes.

There is space in your shoe between your toes; there is a lot more fabric and a lot less bone towards your toes. Look at the portion of the foot labeled "A" in the previous image. This area of your foot is your "broom," and because your "broom" is not very hard, the ball will stop underneath you. Additionally, if you want your first touch to go completely behind you so that you can continue to accelerate away from pressure and into space, then you can take the touch even softer with the inside of your foot towards your toes (i.e., the "broom"). Do this softer than you would if you wanted to stop the ball underneath you. This much softer touch will prevent the ball from racing past you. You can slow it down a little bit but do not stop it entirely because you will attack the space directly behind you.

Tip: Use the inside of your right foot to take a moving first touch to the right and use the inside of your left foot to take a moving first touch to the left. Using the correct foot will make it so that you do not cross your feet, which is incredibly unathletic. Also, you will have more accurate moving first touches when you do not cross your feet.

Coaching Tip: In practice, require that your team "demands" and "yells" for the ball at all times. Even though the passing is in a drill and the players will know exactly where the pass is coming from, have your team establish the habit of always demanding and yelling for the ball, so it will be automatically done in a game. If you are looking for drills with specific coaching points to use in practices in order to increase your player's skills, grab the *Understand Soccer* series book, *Soccer Drills*. By using mental energy to create habits in practice, you will not have to focus on doing so in a game. Creating habits is precisely one of the critical points of practicing; you create the habits to use in a game. After all, it has been said that "perfect practice makes perfect," so expect nothing less than perfection from your team in practices.

YouTube: If you would like to see how to receive the ball effectively in a video format, then consider watching the *Understand Soccer* YouTube video: <u>*How to Improve Your First Touch in Soccer*</u>.

Chapter 10

Weight Training

As an athlete, you should ethically give yourself any possible edge that you can, whether it is strengthening your mindset or improving your knowledge on how to score, defend, run faster, be more explosive, or be tougher to push off the ball, etc. **Likewise, weight training is critical for an athlete to develop excellent abilities off the field that will also be applicable on the field.** It is essential to emphasize moves that are as beneficial as possible but do not consume an excessive amount of time, energy, or emotional capital, which, in the short-term, would take away from training for the game you love. Biceps curls and triceps extensions are not going to make a meaningful difference in your playing career. However, your ability to perform the big three compound lifts will.

The big three are squatting, deadlifting, and bench pressing. Furthermore, since this sport is all about having strong legs, doing some leg presses, calf raises, and lunges will also be very beneficial. You are in a sport that is one of the most calorie-consuming competitions around. Due to all the running, you will expend a lot of calories. Therefore, unless you are a larger soccer player looking to lose weight, spending hours and hours in the weight room is not going to be beneficial for you. However, emphasizing a few key weightlifting moves will be very helpful and will not take that much time to do.

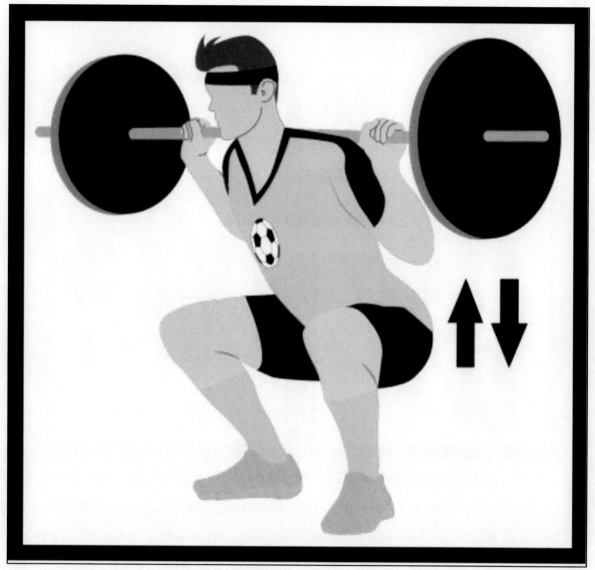

If you have access to a weight room or gym, a move to emphasize and perfect is the **squat**. For this move, the bar is on your back while you are squatting and then standing up again using your hips, quadriceps, hamstrings, and glutes. This lift is known as the king of mass builders and should be a part of all weight lifting routines, as long as there are no previous injuries that prevent the athlete from doing any variation of the squat. If you have previous injuries that prevent certain ranges of motion, attempt all the variations and select the one with which you can use the most weight to work your muscles without causing pain in your joints, ligaments, and tendons. Different variations of the squat are the back squat, front squat, sumo squat, bodyweight/air squat, machine squat, hack squat, kettlebell/goblet squat, Smith Machine squat, Zercher squat, and box squat.

Next, perform the **deadlift** to build overall power. In this move, a bar filled with weight is on the ground. Bend down emphasizing your leg muscles and pick up the weight while driving your hips forward. You may notice that the common theme in these first two lifts is to get your hips working. As an athlete, having strong hips will make you a faster runner, give you strength, make it harder for you to be pushed off the ball, make you much more explosive as you sprint, and it will allow you to shoot more powerful shots.

Additionally, though the **bench press** is not specifically for the lower body, it will help develop your upper body and it will help build confidence. As you begin to gain muscle in your chest, shoulders, and triceps from practicing this move, your self-esteem will soar. A bench press is when you lie with your back on a bench and you press the bar away from your body.

Include **pull-ups** because these are a great exercise to develop your back muscles. These can be done in many places, as long as there is a bar, a tree branch, or a rail, etc. Whether your grip is a reverse grip (i.e., a "chin-up"), neutral grip, narrow grip, standard grip, or wide grip, pull-ups strengthen your back, forearms, and biceps.

Next, if you have access to a gym, **leg presses** are great for adding leg mass and gaining power. To perform a leg press, sit in the machine and use your leg muscles to push the platform. Leg pressing increases your speed and jumping height, as well as how hard you can kick a ball.

Furthermore, **calf raises** are when you push your entire body farther up in the air by moving your ankle and pressing the floor down with the balls of your feet. You can perform calf raises on the leg press platform, with dumbbells in your hands, or with a barbell along your back. It will help you to be more explosive, change direction more quickly, run faster, as well as allowing your body to react more rapidly to the ball.

When you are in the gym, you should emphasize rep ranges of no more than 6 repetitions to develop strength applicable on the field, without packing on muscle size, which will not help you with soccer. Higher rep ranges of 20+ reps will help with your endurance, but you should prioritize gaining more strength. **Emphasizing strength is best done by performing a set of 6 repetitions or less to failure.** Failing within the 8-12 rep range will achieve muscular size (i.e., hypertrophy).

Training for muscular size is not wrong because it will lead to some strength and endurance gains, but it does not directly line up with becoming better as an athlete, if that is your overarching goal. If you do not have access to a gym, some good exercises to perform are squats, lunges, sit-ups, leg raises, planks, push-ups, and supermans. Let us say you are just on the soccer field and it is only you. Squatting or jump squatting will be great for developing leg strength and explosiveness.

Next, **lunging** entails extending one leg in front of your body and one leg behind your body, and then lowering your body into a half-squat with just one leg. When lunging, make sure you do as many reps with your right leg as you do with your left. Similar to squats, you can perform lunges with jumps if they are too easy to do without any additional weight. You can also place your back foot up on something, like the first row of the bleachers or a chair. This becomes what is known as a "Bulgarian split squat." Lifting your leg will give you variation in your lunge and make the lunge more difficult.

Sit-ups are when your upper body hinges up at the waist as you lie on your back. You use your abdominals (i.e., abs) to raise your upper body up. Also, perform leg raises where instead of bringing your upper body up, you bring your legs up. Too many people emphasize sit-ups over leg raises because for leg raises, you have to raise up your legs, which weigh more than your upper body does. Therefore, doing leg raises is going to help you obtain six pack abs a lot quicker than doing sit-ups or crunches will. However, both are important because the sit-ups and crunches emphasize your upper abs whereas the leg raises accentuate the lower abs.

Planks consist of extending your arms straight out (i.e., at the top of the push-up position) or planting your forearms and elbows on the ground while keeping your body straight. A plank works your transverse abdominis, which allows you to work the layer of muscle underneath the abdominal muscles that will be visible once you get six-pack abs. Therefore, planks help you push out your abs, so they become more visible. Developing spectacular abs gives you more confidence, assists with stabilizing your body, and makes you a better athlete.

Push-ups are great to do and similarly to bench pressing, they will develop your pecs (chest), deltoids (shoulders), and triceps (the back of your arms). Though gaining upper body mass is not paramount for this sport, it does boost confidence and increase overall strength. Also, it does not take much additional time to perform a few extra sets on the field after you have done your leg day exercises.

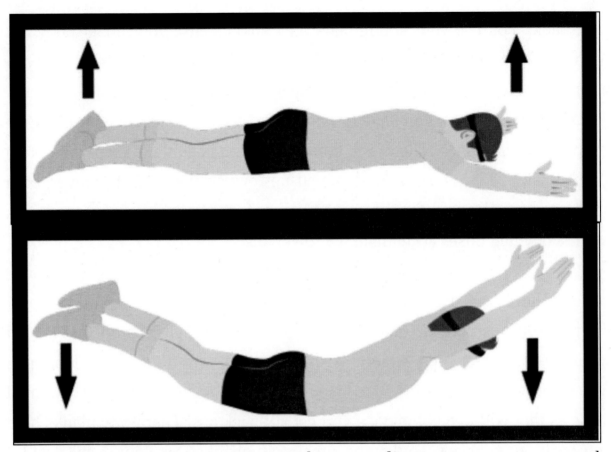

Supermans are an exercise where you lie prone on your stomach. Extend your legs behind you and raise your arms into the air. These are good at developing your glutes, your lower back, shoulders, and your trapezius.

If you do not have a gym where you can add additional weights, and you are just doing these exercises out on the soccer field, doing higher repetitions to failure is going to be much better than not doing it at all or stopping short of failure. It is okay if you are doing push-ups into the 30s or 40s, sit-ups into the 60s or 80s, and many jump squats. Make sure with every exercise that you focus on good form. Weight training is crucial for building confidence. As you gain strength, you will become more confident on the field.

As you exercise and lift more, while making sure that you are consuming more calories, you will start to gain muscle. This will also help boost your self-esteem because you will begin to feel more comfortable and have higher confidence with your body. Yes, it takes time to gain strength and size, but greatness takes time, too. Just by reading this book, you are showing that there is greatness inside you that wants to come out! If you are interested in learning which exercises will give you the best results in the shortest time, how to stretch before a game to avoid decreasing the strength in your legs that so many coaches have their players mistakenly do, or how to run faster, then grab a copy of the *Understand Soccer* series book, *Soccer Fitness: A Step-by-Step Guide on Speed, Endurance, Flexibility, and Strength for a Soccer Player.*

Tip: Always emphasize good form. Similar to completing a drill, you do not want any exercises to be sloppy. Using poor form during push-ups, performing really quick crunches where you are just hurting your neck and back more than actually developing your abs, or performing lazy squats where they only go a quarter of the way down will lead to injuries. Be a stickler for quality over quantity when doing any exercises.

Coaching Tip: Developing the abilities to use in a game is the most important thing to do in practices. Performing passing, dribbling, and attacking drills are more important than focusing on weight training or calisthenics (i.e., bodyweight exercises). However, consider ending a practice with some sprints, squat jumps, split-legged jump lunges, push-ups, sit-ups, leg raises, supermans, planks, or long jumps. **Perform the exercises at the end of your practice because you do not want to tire your players out before you even start training, as it increases the chance of injury.**

YouTube: If you would like to do a workout with instruction from me using only bodyweight exercises, then consider watching the *Understand Soccer* YouTube video: <u>*Soccer Strength Training at Home*</u>.

Chapter 11

Nutrition

As you read this chapter, please understand that I am not a certified dietitian. However, I am a person with tens of thousands of hours of experience on the field, in the weight room, and in the kitchen. Currently, I have read well over 250 nutrition, fitness, bodybuilding, and health magazines, in addition to over 40 nutrition, food science, and weight-training books. Having placed the insights into practice, I have realized that there is much more to be learned in the "doing" than there is in the reading or listening to a subject.

This book provides the understanding, but **the application of the concepts offers in-depth knowledge.** You can understand a lot from reading, but applying what you read is how you take yourself from a novice level to an amateur level, an amateur level to a proficient level, and finally from a proficient level to a professional level.

Let me give you a personal example. I started out as a chubby child, then went to the point of being too skinny because I did not eat enough food, and now I have finally found the sweet spot. I have maintained eight-pack abs for over a decade and definitely have the look of a fit athlete. I state these facts about myself not to brag or impress you but to express that having a good nutrition plan is critical for being healthy, achieving your ideal body, and increasing your performance on the field. With that in mind, countless hours of experimentation and trial-and-error have occurred to develop what works best for me as a soccer player.

Nutrient timing is critical to an athlete. You should not go into a game after drinking half a gallon of milk and eating an entire tub of cottage cheese. You will feel slow; your legs will feel heavier, and you will not perform very well. Also, it is not advisable to go to bed after eating half a loaf of bread and drinking two bottles of soda pop because all the carbohydrates and caffeine will spike your blood sugar and energy levels, which will keep you awake and restless. Additionally, since the meal will not be used to provide needed energy, it will likely be stored as fat. Before bed, you should eat a slower-digesting meal, such as foods that are high in fiber, fat, and protein. Some things to consider consuming are nuts, seeds, meat, and different kinds of nut butters (e.g., almond, cashew, and peanut butter).

Upon awakening in the morning, your body has likely used up most of its glycogen (i.e., blood sugar) throughout the night, so you should consume foods that are higher in carbohydrates. Some examples are fruits, vegetables, and healthy grains, such as quinoa, brown rice, sweet potatoes, steel-cut oatmeal, and organic bread (although bread is not for everyone, considering it has gluten).

These carbohydrates are very beneficial to replenish your glycogen stores and gives you the energy to help you function appropriately until your next meal. Furthermore, there is a common practice in the athletic world that you are supposed to "carb up" the night before a game. Say you have an upcoming game and consume a pasta dinner the night before, to obtain sufficient carbohydrates in your system. However, in reality, you want to eat some carbohydrates, but do not need to eat three bowls of pasta the night before a game.

It will be more beneficial for you to consume carbs closer to the

event, but this depends on how well your body digests food and how empty or full you prefer to be before starting a game. Often, 1-2 hours before a match is an ideal time to take in more carbohydrates in the form of faster-digesting vegetables (e.g., carrots), fruits (e.g., apples, bananas, or watermelon), and carbs (e.g., quinoa, sweet potatoes, or brown rice). If carbs will be consumed immediately before a game, then use faster-digesting carbs, such as white potatoes.

After a game and after exercise, it is ideal to take in nutrition to help build your muscle fibers. You break your muscles down anytime you use them. When they are provided enough quality nutrition and rest, they will grow back stronger. Therefore, when you go to do the same activity, you will be able to perform better, quicker, and more efficiently.

Things that would be good to consume after a physical performance would be foods that are high in carbohydrates and fast-digesting protein. An example that is easy to obtain is organic milk. Though the evidence shows altering views on lactose, having some organic milk after a workout or a whey protein shake with non-GMO dextrose is beneficial. **You want to take in enough carbohydrates to spike up your blood sugar a little bit after a game or workout so that it helps utilize the protein that you will be taking in.**

Whey protein is one of the most bio-available and quickest-digesting proteins that you can use before and after a workout. If you drink milk, it has milk protein, which is 20% whey protein and 80% casein protein. It is essential that you take in enough carbohydrates to replenish your glycogen after a workout if you plan to do more physical activity later in the day. It is critical to minimize the amount of fat and fiber you take in during the 30-minute window after a workout because fiber and fat are slower digesting. They slow the absorption of vitamins, minerals, and nutrients. You should also avoid very dense foods, like spinach or peanut butter—unless there is absolutely nothing else that you can consume. After all, something healthy is better than nothing.

When it comes to nutrition, you have likely heard it before a hundred times that "you are what you eat." Something that you may have never heard or read is that **you are what your food eats** too. Therefore, it is vital that you have high-quality food. If the cow, chicken, pig, turkey, or fish that you are eating is consuming nutritious food too, those animals will provide more value than other poorly fed animals.

Having food that you know is eating other living organisms and healthy food, you will have much more vitamin-rich, nutrient-dense, mineral-packed food. Healthy food is in direct opposition to the salmon that is farm-raised eating soy pellets, the chicken that is caged, and the cow that is eating a mix of canola meal and cottonseed hulls. These types of animal meats provide lackluster nutrition that will give you the same amount of protein, fat, and carbohydrates. However, concerning the higher levels of nutrition (e.g., the vitamins, minerals, nutrients, antioxidants, phytonutrients, and even more things about food that have not been discovered yet) they will be lacking.

Not all vegetables are created equal. Though plants do not eat other food, they do absorb nutrients from the soil, and genetically modified foods lack the rich nutrients you need from fruits, vegetables, and grains. Genetically modified foods have had their organic structure altered to withstand harmful weed killers, such as glyphosate. The most genetically modified foods on the market are sugar, canola, cottonseed, soy, squash, zucchini, alfalfa, and corn.

Many countries around the world have already banned glyphosate, but at the time of writing this book, it is still not banned in the United States of America. It helps to kill weeds that are competing for the same nutrition in the soil as the cultivated crop. **Though having fewer weeds is good in theory, using harmful and synthetic weed killers to do so is not good.** The glyphosate acts as a mineral chelator making it so that the plant does not take the nutrients, vitamins, and minerals from the soil at the rate that it would have if the soil had not been sprayed with that mineral chelator. Therefore, you will have the same amount of protein, fat, and carbohydrates from a genetically modified ear of corn versus a non-genetically modified ear of corn, however, the genetically modified corn is going to have a lot less nutritional value that is very important for an athlete. If you have ever been sluggish in a game, wanted to know exactly what to eat before a game to give you the most energy, or wanted to know what to consume after a match to ensure you gain muscle and help recovery, then grab a copy of the *Understand Soccer* series book, *Soccer Nutrition*.

Finally, one of the most important things for an athlete is a minimum of seven quality hours of sleep per night. If you want to learn how to fall asleep quickly and stay asleep all night so that you can wake up feeling very well-rested and energized the next day, then grab a copy of the *Understand Soccer* series book, *Soccer Sleep: A Step-by-Step Guide on How to Get a Good Night's Sleep Every Single Night.*

Parenting Tip: Players need at least 7 hours and at most 9 hours of sleep. **Countless studies have shown that more or less can lead to a lack of motivation, energy, and awareness.** To ensure that it is good-quality sleep, turn off any additional lights in the room and eliminate as much noise as possible. Make sure your child affirms to themselves that they are a good sleeper. This will improve their quality and quantity of sleep. Remember that this starts with you. If you have a habit of talking about how bad at sleeping you are, your child will likely adopt your mindset and consider themselves to be bad at sleeping, too.

Coaching Tip: Make sure that your team can replenish their glycogen levels to ensure they have enough stored energy to perform in the next game for any tournaments or days with long practices. Grab several bananas, a bag of apples, or other fruits. Additionally, having a gallon of milk on ice and a few Dixie cups with you to pour some post-game nutrition after the last game of the day will definitely make a difference in your team's recovery and performance.

YouTube: If you would like to see what to eat before a game or practice, then consider watching the *Understand Soccer* YouTube video: *What to Eat Before a Soccer Game*.

Chapter 12

Stretching & Flexibility

Flexibility is significant for longevity in any athletic endeavor. However, the type of stretching that you should do depends on the kind of exercise you will be doing or have already completed. **Before strenuous training, you should engage in dynamic stretching.** Dynamic stretching involves shaking your muscles out, performing jumping jacks, and doing other movements to push the synovial fluid into your joints and increase the blood flow to your muscles.

The objective is to have your muscles ready to engage in physical activity. **It is crucial that you do not hold any stretches/poses for anything more than a few seconds because it will decrease power output by up to 10% during your athletic performance.** Therefore, you would be spending time before an athletic event to reduce your performance by holding long/static stretches before you exercise. Other high-quality movements that are perfect before physical activity, given no previous injuries, are mild jogging that speeds up to fast jogging that then becomes sprinting as your body starts to become warmed up. Furthermore, focusing on jumping and the progression of passing a ball, then softly shooting a shot, and then striking the ball with full power is excellent for warming up before a game too. Any warm-up you do, you want to start with the easiest form of that movement and then build your way up to the harder versions, the more game-like versions. You never want to start with sprinting for the beginning of your warm-up. It is better to have a nice and easy walk that turns into a jog that then becomes a few sprints.

It is appropriate to perform static stretches after a practice or

game. At this point, your body is fatigued, warm, supple, and flexible because you were just exercising. You are not worried about power output anymore because you have already completed your practice or game. Now, it is time to focus on deep stretches that will improve the longevity of your joints, as well as increase your muscle length to allow you to feel better, recover faster, and play the sport you love for longer.

Most athletes, especially early in their career, tend to avoid stretching because it just really does not seem like it contributes that much. This mindset and lack of action is a very nearsighted way to look at your overall game. It is not necessary to spend 30 minutes warming up before a game and another 30 minutes cooling down after a game. **However, it is suggested that you take 5-10 minutes before you will start striking a ball or begin playing in a game.**

Cool down after a game. Pick a few basic stretches to perform for your hamstrings, quadriceps, glutes, hip flexors, adductors, abductors, and calves. Have one exercise or one stretch for each one of those muscles at a minimum, which you perform after your athletic performance and have it as a routine/habit that you do after every single game. After the first few times you stretch, you will not even have to think about it anymore. A consistent theme throughout this entire book is to create the habit of the important things so that the habit can create the future you. It will take some mental effort to establish these. However, once you set them up, they become natural, and you almost feel like something is missing when you do not do them. Frequently, you go on autopilot to where you are not even aware that you are doing them until you are more than halfway through the stretches.

You should also perform dynamic stretching before any weight training. You should never start with your maximum bench press weight on the bar. You should start with just the bar, and then add weight to each side in increments until your body, joints, and muscles feel ready to engage fully in the exercise.

Spending a few minutes warming up before exercise and cooling down after physical activity helps make sure that your body stays fit and healthy. You should always choose to warm up before you play and remember that you are not truly done until after you cool down. Include static stretches at the end of any workout to make sure that you are improving your flexibility and reducing your chances of injury.

Tip: Using one or both arms while standing, pull one foot behind your body (i.e., to where you are bending at the knee). This will stretch your quadriceps (i.e., the muscles along the front of your thighs). While standing, put one ankle over your opposite knee and push on the knee of your bent leg to stretch your glutes (i.e., your buttocks) and your abductors (i.e., the muscles along the outside of your thighs). Keeping both feet on the ground and reaching down (i.e., bending to touch your toes) will stretch your hamstrings (i.e., the muscles along the back of your thighs).

Sitting on the ground and pulling your ankles between your legs while bending at the knees and pushing your elbows against your knees will stretch your adductors (i.e., the muscles along the inside of your thighs). Go into a lunge and put the knee of your back leg on the ground while driving your hips towards the floor. Using your arms to push against the knee in front of you, push your upper body backward to stretch out your hip flexor (i.e., the muscles atop the front of your thighs, where your hips are). In a plank position, drive your hips backward. This is like going into downward dog, but only on the balls of your feet. Now, place one ankle on top of the other. Push yourself towards the space behind you to stretch your calves (i.e., the muscles that run along the back of your legs, below your knees).

Coaching Tip: Make sure that you start every practice with dynamic stretches and end with static stretches. Do this along with your players to **lead by example** and improve your overall health and well-being. Make sure to keep relatively the same stretching routine before and after games so that your team can become mentally focused and physically ready for each practice or game.

YouTube: If you would like to see how to stretch before a game, then consider watching the *Understand Soccer* YouTube video: *Stretching Before a Soccer Game*.

Chapter 13

Juggling

Juggling should be done to develop skills that are applicable on the field. **Although being able to do an "around-the-world" with a ball is glamorous and fun, it does not often carry over well into a game.** I have played with many players who were great jugglers but had a terrible first touch and were not so good on the field. Therefore, when you juggle, make sure it is to become better with your in-game abilities. For the readers who are looking to become better defenders, midfielders, forwards, or goalies, juggling is a way to get touches on the ball and use the top side of your foot.

When juggling, be sure to juggle the ball so that it has either no spin or a bit of backspin. This will make it easier. If you put a forward spin on the ball, you will constantly have to reach for the ball to make sure that your foot is underneath it. Additionally, make sure to emphasize both feet—especially your opposite foot—because a good soccer player uses both feet. Developing only one foot will make a career in this wonderful sport much more difficult.

When you practice juggling, do not try to obtain a higher number of juggles using mostly your thighs (as shown in the picture). You are rarely going to use the portion of your body above your knees in a game. Therefore, if you practice juggling with your thighs, you are spending quality practice time inefficiently. Be logical about juggling, because your juggles should be similar to the touches that you will take in a game. Use the top side of your foot to get an efficient first touch and settle the ball out of the air.

Parenting Tip: Ensure that when your child is juggling, they are using a goals-based approach. A goals-based approach means that your child should not just juggle to juggle. Instead, help them set a measurable goal. **Having a measurable goal will make your child's improvement much more realistic and something they can work on achieving.** Saying, "I want to juggle a lot for a long time" is not measurable enough. Instead, they should increase their ability to juggle by setting a goal like, "Yesterday, I reached 60 juggles. Today, I want to reach 65." Setting goals that are measurable will allow your child to quickly determine whether they met their goal or not.

Coaching Tip: Communicate to your players that standing with the ball at their feet without developing their skills is wasteful. While your players are waiting in line for their turn to dribble through a set of cones is an ideal time for them to work on their juggling. However, juggling should only be practiced when they are waiting because practice time is better spent working on their first touch, attacking with the ball, developing their foot skills, or working on their shot.

YouTube: If you want to learn some easy juggling tricks, then consider watching the *Understand Soccer* YouTube video: *Juggling Tricks to Impress Your Friends*.

Chapter 14

Soccer Mindset

In both soccer and in life, you can do whatever you put your mind to —as long as you take the actions to back up your decisions. To be a useful player, it is essential that you do not carry any limiting beliefs. **Some examples of limiting beliefs are "I am not good with my left foot," "I cannot score," or "I am not that fast."** It is important that your ideas fully align with the person and player you want to become. A simple change in mindset and some follow-up actions will make a massive difference in your career.

Do not ever say that you have a "weak foot." If you are not as good with your left foot, call it your "opposite foot," so you have a "strong foot" and an "opposite foot." Also, saying that "I am not fast" will pretty much ensure that you never become fast. Keep in mind, as discussed in other chapters, that being a fast soccer player is as much about your first touch and your ability to control the ball as it is about you being able to sprint without the ball. Sure, you may never get to the point to where you are winning 50-yard sprints against Usain Bolt, but limiting yourself from the beginning by saying that you are not fast will make it so that you never become fast. It ensures that you do not do the steps of squatting, deadlifting, sprinting, and additional training that allows you to become faster.

Furthermore, telling yourself, "I cannot score," and "I am not good at scoring" will prevent you from seeking out the knowledge you need to learn how to become a good scorer. Reading books and watching videos is an efficient way to shorten your learning curve and become better quickly. Anytime you play soccer on any team, there are always going to be people who can play defense and midfield. However, a person who can consistently score is uncommon. Knowing that you can score will give you so much confidence in your game that you will never again want to limit your mindset by saying that you cannot perform one of the most essential skills in the game.

There are many more limiting beliefs in the game than the ones mentioned previously, such as your size, your height, or your newness to the sport. **Make sure that anything that holds you back within your mind, you reframe in a way that will make you better and strive for greatness.** Therefore, you may not be as good with your opposite foot as you want to be, but it will help to rephrase it as "I am working to get there. I will be there with knowledge, time, and persistence." Say "I may not currently a fast runner, but that does not keep me from being a fast soccer player nor does that keep me from training to become a faster runner, while gaining the knowledge to do so." Say "though I do not score many goals currently in a game, I will work to gain information of tips, tricks, and tactics to take better shots, to beat more defenders, and shoot with more accuracy and power." If you are interested in learning more about how to master your mindset and what attitudes it will take to win, then grab a copy of the *Understand Soccer* series book, *Soccer Mindset: A Step-by-Step Guide on How to Outsmart Your Opponents and Improve Your Mentality.*

YouTube: If you would like to see a video to improve your mindset, then consider watching the *Understand Soccer* YouTube video: Soccer Training the Mind - Growth vs Fixed Mindset.

Parenting Tip: Being around other negative players can make your child a bit more negative, too. Let us be honest; we have all played with or have a child who has played with someone who plays only for themselves and blames everyone else for anything that goes wrong. This kind of behavior is counterproductive to the team's goals, so work with your child to help improve their mindset and keep them from falling into this bad habit. Keep up your positivity and encourage others around you, including your child. **Guard your mind, and your child's mind against the negative people on their team.**

Coaching Tip: Make sure that your players remove any negative thoughts on the field or off. However, you must also make sure that you do not get mad at your players if they tell you about their limiting beliefs. **Getting mad will make it worse.** Your players may feel like you are patronizing or condescending to them if you attempt to correct their mindsets. Instead, let them know that you used to be that way, too. Say, "I used to have limiting beliefs that held me back. Because of my limiting beliefs, it took longer to become the player I wanted to be. But when I changed my mindset, I became the player I truly wanted to be. I am not perfect, either, but with a few modifications to your mindset and your form, you will be a great soccer player, too!"

Also, work on having your players realize that positivity does not make things easier, but it makes everything *seem* easier. Trevor Moawad is a mental conditioning expert and strategic advisor to many of the world's most elite performers. He was named the "Sports World's Best Brain Trainer" by Sports Illustrated in 2017, and he says that **negativity is 4-7X as powerful as positivity**. In fact, he has worked directly with Nick Saban, the Alabama football coach, to help their program become arguably the best college football program in the nation in the decade of the 2010s. His best coaching point at Alabama was to get the players on the team to not say anything negative. They can think it, but they are not allowed to verbalize it to other players because negativity is contagious, saps players of their energy, and makes kids fearful of making mistakes. Therefore, take this same mindset to your team and insist that negativity not be spoken out loud. If you are interested in learning more about how negativity will ruin your player's minds and how to train your players to avoid it, then grab a copy of the *Understand Soccer* series book, *Soccer Drills*.

become a goal-scorer who averages about two goals and an assist per game—all because he increased his understanding of how to play soccer. With the help of a soccer mentor, he took his game from being a bench-warmer who got called out in front of everybody to becoming the most confident player on the field.

Currently, he is a soccer trainer in Michigan, working for Next Level Training. He advanced through their rigorous program as a soccer player and was hired as a trainer. This program has allowed him to guide world-class players for over a decade in formats ranging from one-hour classes to weeklong camps, and he instructs classes of all sizes, from groups of 30 soccer players all the way down to working one-on-one with individuals wanting to play for the United States National Team.

If you enjoyed this book, then please leave a review.

Dedication

This book is dedicated to all the soccer players, coaches, and parents who want to improve their knowledge and strengthen others around them. Whether it be for yourself, your team, or your child, striving to grow in order to help others and yourself develop is exceptionally noble and speaks volumes about the person you are.

Glossary

50-50 - When a ball is passed into pressure or cleared up the field and your teammate and a player on the opposing team each have an equal (50%) chance of taking possession of the ball.

Ball Hawk - Someone usually close to the ball, in the right place at the right time, and a person who specializes in scoring rebounds.

Bat - The bone (i.e., hardest portion) of your foot.

Bent/Curved Shot - A shot that spins and curves as it goes towards the net. This shot is used when you need to shoot around defenders or goalkeepers. Though you use the bone of your foot to strike the ball instead of following through the ball with your entire body, you just follow through with your leg and cross your legs after shooting the ball.

Bicycle Kick (i.e., "Overhead Kick") - where the ball is above you and you proceed to jump up and kick the ball over your body while the ball is in the air.

Body Feint (i.e., "Feint," "Fake," "Fake and Take," "Jab Step," or "Shoulder Drop") - When you pretend to push the ball in one direction, but purposely miss, then plant with the same foot and then push the ball in the other direction with the opposite foot.

Broom - In this book, it is the area on your foot towards your toes. There is space in your shoe between your toes where there is a lot more fabric and a lot less bone, which makes it a soft area on your foot, similar to the softness of a broom.

Champions League - The UEFA Champions League is an annual soccer competition involving the best of the best club teams from many of the professional leagues in Europe.

Chop - This is performed with the outside of your foot. The leg that is cutting the ball must step entirely past the ball. Then, allow the ball to hit that leg/foot, which effectively stops the ball. Having the ball stop next to your foot enables the ball to be pushed in a different direction quickly.

Counterattack (i.e., "Fast Break") - When the team defending gains possession of the ball and quickly travels up the field with the objective of taking a quick shot, so few of the other team's players can travel back to defend in time.

Crossbar Challenge - Played by one or more people where you attempt to hit the crossbar by shooting the ball from the 18-yard box.

Cruyff - When you cut the ball but leave yourself between the defender and the ball. In essence, you are cutting the ball behind your planted leg.

Cut - This is performed with the inside of your foot. The leg that is cutting the ball must step entirely past the ball. Then, allow the ball to hit that leg/foot, which effectively stops the ball. Having the ball stop next to your foot enables the ball to be pushed in a different direction quickly. Additionally, you may cut the ball so that it is immediately moving in the direction that you want to go.

Driven Shot (i.e., "Sledgehammer Shot") - A shot struck with the bone of your foot, where you follow through with your entire body without crossing your legs. This is the most powerful type of shot.

Finishing - The purpose of shooting which is to score.

Flick - Barely touching the ball to change the direction of the ball slightly for a teammate when a pass is being played to you.

Half-Volley - Striking the ball just after it hit the ground, but while the ball is still in the air.

Jockeying - When defending, backpedaling to maintain proper position in relation to the person attacking with the ball. When jockeying, the defender does not dive in for the ball. He or she waits for the ideal time to steal the ball or poke it away.

Jump Turn - Instead of pulling the ball back with the bottom of your foot, as you would do in the V pull back, stop the ball with the bottom of your foot as you jump past the ball, landing with both feet at the same time on the other side of the ball. Landing with both feet at the same time on the other side of the ball allows you to explode away in the direction from which you came.

Moving First Touch (i.e., "Attacking Touch") - Pushing the ball into space with your first touch, which is the opposite of taking a touch where the ball stops underneath you (i.e., at your feet).

Offside - When you pass the ball to a player on your team who is past the opposing team's last defender at the moment the kick is initiated. You cannot be offside on a throw-in or when you are on your own half of the field.

One-Time Shot - When a pass or cross is played to you and your first touch is a shot on net.

Opposite Foot - Your non-dominant foot. Out of your two feet, it is the one that you are not as comfortable using.

Outside of the Foot Shot (i.e., "Trivela") - Shooting with the bone of your foot where your toe is pointed down and in. The ball makes contact with the outside portion/bone of your foot. This shot is useful because it is quicker than a driven shot, it can provide bend like a bent shot, and is more powerful than a pass shot.

Pass Fake - When you fake a pass. Make sure to keep your form the same as when you actually make a pass. This includes: (1) looking at a teammate before you do a pass fake; and (2) raising your passing leg high enough behind your body so that your opponent believes you are going to kick the ball.

Pass Shot (i.e., "Finesse Shot" or "Instep Drive") - A shot on the net using the inside of your foot to increase your accuracy. Make sure to land past the ball on the follow-through to increase the shot's power, similar to a shot taken with the bone of your foot.

Passing Lane - An area on the field where a teammate can pass you the ball directly, while the ball remains on the ground.

Pitch - A soccer field.

Rainbow - When you place one foot in front of the ball and the laces of the other foot behind the ball. Pin the ball between your feet and flick the ball up behind your body and over your head.

Roll (i.e., "Rollover") - Using the bottom of the toes of your foot, roll the ball parallel to the defender, crossing your feet when you plant. Then, bring your other foot around to uncross your feet and push the ball forward. The path the ball takes is the shape of an "L."

Self-Pass (i.e., "L," "Iniesta," or "La Croqueta") - Passing the ball from one foot to the other while running. Imagine you are doing a roll, but without your foot going on top of the ball. Instead, it is an inside of the foot pass from one foot and an inside of the foot push up the field with the other foot.

Set Piece (i.e., "Dead Ball") - A practiced plan used when the ball goes out of bounds or a foul is committed to put the ball back into play. The most common set pieces are throw-ins and free kicks.

Scissor - When your foot closest to the ball goes around the ball as you are attacking a defender in a game. Emphasize turning your hips to fake the defender. To easily turn your hips, plant past the ball with your foot that is not going around the ball so that you can use the momentum of the moving ball to your advantage.

Shielding - Placing your body between the ball and the defender. With your back facing the defender and your arms wide, prevent them from traveling to the ball.

Shot Fake - Faking a shot. Make sure your form looks the same as when you shoot, including: 1) Looking at the goal before you do a shot fake 2) Arms out 3) Raise your shooting leg high enough behind your body, so it looks like you are going to shoot.

Square to Your Teammate - Pointing your hips at a teammate.

Step-On-Step-Out - To change direction, step on the ball with the bottom of your foot. Then, with the same foot, take another step and plant to the side of the ball, so that your other leg can come through and push the ball in a different direction.

Step-Over - When you are next to the ball and you have your farthest leg from the ball step over the ball, so your entire body turns as if you are going in a completely different direction. The step over is best used along a sideline.

Through Ball/Run - When a pass is played into space in front of you, allowing you to continue your forward momentum.

Toe Poke/Toe Blow - Striking the ball with your big toe. The toe poke is the quickest shot, but often the most inaccurate shot.

Upper 90 - Either of the top corners on a net (i.e., corners are 90 degrees).

V Pull Back - Pull the ball backward using the bottom of your foot. Then, use your other leg to push the ball and accelerate forward in the other direction, hence the "V" in the V pull back.

Volley - Striking the ball out of the air before it hits the ground.

Wall Passing (i.e., "1-2 Passing" or "Give-and-Go") - When you pass to a teammate, and they pass back to you with one touch. This is similar to passing a ball against a wall.